I I

SCONES

Deedee Cuddihy

First Published 2023
Copyright©2023 by Deedee Cuddihy

ISBN 978 0 9930986 97

Published by Deedee Cuddihy
10 Otago Street,
Glasgow G12 8JH
Scotland

Cover design, technical and research assistance: The Lodger (Glasgow) Ltd.

Printed by Bell and Bain Ltd, Glasgow

Dedication

This book is dedicated to Irvines Bakery, the Ayrshire company whose fabulous treacle scone, purchased at their Kilbirnie branch (for a mere 60 pence, butter included) persuaded me that scones were, indeed, a subject worth pursuing. And many thanks to all my contributors including Barbara, Baroness Young of Old Scone (pronounced "scoon") whose response to my email far exceeded expectations.

Foreword

Until I began research for this book, I had no idea that people could be so passionate about . . . scones! My ignorance was obviously due to the fact that I was brought up in a sconeless country (the USA) and didn't eat my first scone until I moved to Scotland, at age 14, more than 50 years ago. Mrs. Moore, the chain-smoking cook at the eccentric boarding school I went to, could be seen most days stirring up batches of scones in the kitchen, a tipped cigarette waggling at the corner of her mouth, an inch of fag ash threatening to land in the mix at any moment. I've made my own scones since then, not realising there was a level of scone expertise I should have been aiming for. But it was only when I noticed that they appeared to have beome trendy - even hipster cafes in my area of Glasgow were serving them - that my interest in scones was piqued. All of my face-to-face research was carried out in Scotland but the people I spoke to came, not just from most areas of the UK but from all over the world. Talking to people is always fascinating but for this book, there were added scones.

PEOPLE ARE VERY PASSIONATE ABOUT SCONES

and, to be fair, we do have good scones. I've eaten a couple on the rare occasion when we've had some left over at closing time. And we sometimes offer them to customers as well - so there's a tip for you! Our scones are fresh baked here but you can only make so many because you don't want a lot left over at the end of the day. They don't keep; you can't eat a day-old scone.

(member of staff at the M&S cafe in Glasgow where, to the chagrin of at least one customer, the scones had run out on a Saturday afternoon)

"I look forward to having a scone here on a Saturday afternoon and this is the third Saturday in a row that there've been no scones left! Can you not just make more? Or could I not phone up and reserve one?"

(Woman in an M&S cafe in Glasgow having a meltdown due to a lack of scones - but who eventually settled for a toasted tea cake.)

JEAN AND HAZEL ARE FRIENDS AND SCONE AFICIONADOS FROM PRESTWICK, IN AYRSHIRE.

They often go out together and have a scone at a cafe. They say: "A scone has to be moist and cut nicely when you slice into it. And they're no good the next day, unless you toast them." Jean: "I don't make scones now but I used to make them with my daughter, and have them with Golden Syrup which was delicious." They say: "Making scones was just something that your mum and granny did when we were growing up." Jean: "I can remember that, if her scones hadn't turned out the right way, my mum would say they were Rock Cakes, as if she'd done it on purpose!" Hazel: "I've always got some scones in the freezer if visitors come. I don't make them myself now because you can buy a packet in the shops for under £2. You just put them under the grill." Jean: "I really like a treacle scone but not a fruit one. And there's nothing worse when you're out and get a scone and there's cheap jam with it. It ruins it." Neither of them likes cherry scones because they don't like glace cherries. And they don't like the new types of scones, for instance date and walnut which they came across in a garden centre cafe. "Fine as a cake or a bread" they say "but not a scone."

(the author met Jean and Hazel at the Maclaurin Art Gallery in Ayr)

In prison, for your supper at night, you'd get given a mug of tea and a scone. They must have taken them straight from the freezer and not heated them up because they were as hard as bricks. We called them rock cakes.

(Tommy)

"A rolling scone gathers no moss"

At the Young Farmers club I was a member of in Carrick, we had competitions every year and one of them was for Best Baker which you had to make scones for. The year my brother was chairman, I won it! And because it was tradition that the chairman's mother presented the prizes, I got my prize from my mum. No, it wasn't a fix! I deserved to get my name on that cup. I made scones after I got married and my mother made scones, probably at least every second day, when we were growing up on the farm. Farmers are always starving and we ate scones anytime, with butter and jam. They were always available.

(Morag, 83)

I never made scones when my husband was alive because his were so good - especially the treacle ones. Then I started making cheese scones during lockdown, using a recipe book I got when we were first married - more than 40 years ago. They say you need a light hand when you're making scones and after the second or third attempt, mine were great! But I had to stop making them because I put on so much weight.

(Liz)

If I ever came home with a pack of scones that I'd bought in a shop, my (late) mum would go absolutely berserk - like Linda Blair in the The Exorcist when her head spins 'round. She'd say: ***"They're the easiest thing in the world to make!"*** Sunday was her baking day and her scones were delicious. I always used her recipe for making scones - until I came across the one by Gary Rhodes which is even better than hers. So, if you're listening, Mum - I'm sorry!

(Robert, antiques dealer)

Our next-door-neighbour, a former theatre nurse, is 91 and a few months after her husband died, she began socialising again by inviting a few friends over for an afternoon scone baking session. She told us that they'd often said how good her scones were so she decided to teach them to make their own. She had the kitchen set up like a home economics classroom, with all the equipment and an apron and notebook and pencil laid out for each guest. And she told them the scone making must be done in complete silence - absolutely no talking! So it was deadly serious. But once the scones were in the oven, the gin was brought out and they all had a drink! She's held several more baking sessions since then and at the last one, she told us they drank two bottles of champagne when the scones were in the oven!

(Stella and Gordon)

"Leave no scone unturned"

I'd like to say that it was an ordinary scone, spread with butter and jam and secured in a paper bag, that my mum used to throw out the window to me when I was playing down in the backcourt of the tenement we lived in in Scotstoun - a very nice, red sandstone tenement, by the way - but it was actually a *soda* scone which is more robust than an ordinary scone which would have been too fragile to be flung out a window and would probably have fallen apart.

(Jane)

I like a cheese scone - I made some cheese and chive ones recently. I don't put anything on a scone, not even butter - it masks the taste All that talk about a "perfect scone" and not touching the dough too much or getting too much air into it . . . it's nonsense! When I worked for Prudential in their Stirling office, the staff canteen had scones that were so good, you had to get there early in the morning or else they'd be sold out. I could never understand why they didn't just make more. If I'd already had breakfast, I'd get one for later on and heat it up in the office microwave.

(Naomi)

I blurted out: *"That's not right!"* when a customer asked for butter *and* cream with her scone the other day.

I shouldn't have said that but I couldn't help it. I've made a lot of scones. We had to make them at school in Blackpool where I grew up, as well as rock cakes and button biscuits - have you heard of those? - and when I was working flipping property with my ex-fiancee, who was Irish, he used to come home for lunch with his brother from their building jobs and, during my break from knocking down walls, I'd have made them three scones each and a pot of tea. These days, I'll have a fruit scone occasionally - with cream - but my husband's French and a pain aux raisins would be more his thing.

(Glasgow cafe manager)

"THAT'S FIGHTING TALK WHERE I COME FROM!"

This was the indignant response from Will, a native of North Carolina in the US, when asked if what are called Southern Biscuits in his neck of the woods aren't very like . . . scones. It transpires that folk from that part of America are very passionate, and protective, about their Southern Biscuits although once he'd simmered down, Will who's lived and worked in Glasgow for many years, did concede that the food tastes of Scots and Southerners are similar - and that his beloved "biscuits" might have had their genuses in the scone tradition that Scottish immigrants brought with them when they settled in the south. He said: "Biscuits are an everyday staple in the southern states. My mother and my grandmother made them but, like scones, not everyone is good at making them; the same ingredients are used but not with a standard result." Will added: "You know what the perfect breakfast is? A biscuit - just spread with butter, nothing else - and a cup of coffee. We've also got the Sausage Biscuit which is, yes, very similar to a roll and sausage."

*"**B**ut then there are those biscuits - American scones anyone? - with more gloop (sausage gravy). These I'm not so sure about. A little bit stodgy, perhaps. An acquired taste?"*

(Ron McKenna, reviewing a southern soul food restaurant in Glasgow for the Herald, 2023)

"Sconnae no dae that?"

I wasn't familiar with scones until we moved to Scotland.

I'm French and you wouldn't find scones in France although we've embraced brownies and chocolate chip cookies. But when I'd been here for a while, I realised that scones reminded me of the Southern Biscuits we had in Athens, Georgia in the US when we moved there for several years for my husband's job. I learned to make Southern biscuits and they're delicious. They're a savoury thing that you have along with a meal and you don't eat them with cream or jam - but maybe butter. And you could buy a breakfast of a Southern biscuit with fried chicken inside, like a sandwich. I still make them from time to time, for instance if we're celebrating Thanksgiving, because my son, who is 19, loves them.

(Lucie)

******

A French couple came into the hotel one day - it was mid morning - and asked if they could have coffee and croissants. I said: "I'm sorry but here in Scotland we only have the Scone." So they ended up with two of our freshly baked scones, with butter and jam, and pronounced them delicious - of course!"

(Rosemary Brown of the Copy and Print Shop in Glasgow and erstwhile owner of the Allan Ramsay Hotel)

I've heard about scones - on a Chinese social media platform. I was reading about scones just this morning! You eat them with clotted cream and strawberry jam. I've never had one. This student said they were very good and that she was making them back in China, since she's returned home from the UK.

(Chinese student at Glasgow University)

"Feed two birds with one scone"
(PETA's animal-friendly version of the well-known saying)

"I'm from Nigeria and I hadn't eaten a scone until I moved to Scotland several years ago but now I love them and eat them in the morning with a cup of coffee. I have a friend, Agnes, from Malawi, who is a great baker and her scones are particularly good."

(Israel, a volunteer at the community cafe in Wellington Church in Glasgow where students and others from abroad can practice their English.)

"Do we have any thoughts about scones? You've asked the right people because we're Devon girls! And Devon is the home of the cream tea."

A cream tea, they explain, is a scone with clotted cream and jam, and probably a pot of tea. "It's something you have between lunch and dinner, often in a cafe. Everyone in Devon eats scones, young and old people; it's part of our food culture. We don't often make scones ourselves although we learned to make them at school, in Home Economics. Do we eat scones with butter? No - not unless it's maybe a cheese scone. Clotted cream is instead of butter. And scones should be eaten on the day they're made - as fresh as possible." There's great rivalry, they say, between Devon and Cornwall, in terms of what you put on a scone first - the cream or the jam. Bryony: *"Jam first, definitely."* Beth: *"Cream first."* What type of jam? Bryony: *"Strawberry."* Beth: *"Raspberry jam is better."*

Fact: Devon is cream first; Cornwall is jam first.

(these Devon girls, in their early 20s, first met when studying at Glasgow University and spoke to the author in the city's Partick Library, where they were both working)

I remember being on holiday in St. Ives in Cornwall years ago, when my daughter was about six, and I was cycling back, with her in the child seat, to the caravan we were staying in, and we came to this farm cottage - I think it was called "The Wink" * - and it had a sign up saying "Cream Teas". We were quite hungry by then so I stopped and the woman who ran it baked the scones fresh for us and we got *three each*, with cream and jam. They were delicious!

(Karen)

*Winks were a kind of establishment in Cornwall that fell somewhere between a house and a pub and had different licensing regulations as such. (from the internet)

My cousin and I took the kids down to Cornwall years ago for a holiday and we'd get a cream tea each from a carry out place, spread a blanket on the sand and have it right on the beach - a pot of tea and a scone with jam and cream. We did that almost every day for two weeks. It was great! We had to make scones at school in home economics and when I brought them home for my parents they said: *"Oh - lovely!"* but they were like rock cakes!

(Lorraine)

I made scones once. We got basic stuff like that in Home Economics at high school, and you'd take home what you'd made. I can't remember what the family thought - it was almost 40 years ago! I wouldn't go out of my way for a scone but I ate quite a few when I was based in Devon with the Marines - you know, a Cream Tea with the scones and the jam and the clotted cream. And you can split a cold scone in half, stick it under the grill, and then spread it with a bit of butter.

(Ed)

Oh - we ate scones in Ireland; of course we did!

And we learned how to make them at school - there were only girls in the home economics class - where we were taught by the awful Mrs. Flannery. She was a horror and was still wearing those long, pink bloomers under her skirt in the 1970s! However, in winter, when it was freezing, she'd turn all the electric ovens on and let us sit around them, getting a heat, while she taught the lesson. I make scones sometimes. My mummy made wonderful scones. She wouldn't use one of those round metal cutters because she said it

knocked the air out of them. Instead,
she used the edge of a thin, china
plate to cut the dough into squares.
She said it was quicker than a knife.
And if we had visitors, she'd cut the
scone dough into diagonal shapes
instead of squares and we got the left
over bits. I like a fruit scone. You see
people putting jam on a fruit scone
which is bad on every level. The only
tolerable thing to put on a fruit scone
is lemon curd.

(Carol)

The Hairy Bikers have a really
good tip for scone makers: instead
of using a cookie cutter - or similar
- on the dough after you've patted
it out, roll it up and slice it into
scones with a knife instead, thus
eliminating the *mutant scone* that's
always left when you use the
cookie cutter method.

(Kirsty Miller, actor/book seller)

We don't have scones in Nova Scotia, where I'm from.

The nearest thing to a scone would be Nova Scotia oatcakes which are more like flapjacks. I ate a lot of them in high school. But I stopped eating gluten before moving to Glasgow eight years ago so I haven't tried a proper scone. I know you can get gluten-free scones in a packet from supermarkets but I've yet to come across a freshly baked one in a cafe which seems unfair! I did try to make some scones using chickpea flour but they weren't a success. And our baby sitter, Martin, made some gluten free scones which were good, eaten with a lot of butter, but not as puffy as a normal scone.

(Emily, musician, composer and animal song researcher)

******

Just had a gluten-free scone in the M&S cafe. It wasn't nearly as awful as I had anticipated, although in a blind tasting - that is, literally with a blindfold on - I don't think I would necessarily have identified it as a scone. It was sweeter than a normal scone with quite a solid texture and lots of sultanas. I ate it cold, straight from the packet with no butter or jam.

(from a text)

HOLY SCONES!

We've got a supporter who makes scones once a month for the community Sunday Feast at our Hare Krishna centre in Cardiff where I'm based. The food we offer is mostly Indian apart from the scones which are served with butter and jam as dessert. She must have baked at least a thousand scones in the time she's been coming to the centre - where she also meditates - and, along with token portions of the other food that's going to be served at the feast, **a scone is brought to the altar on a tray and offered up to Lord Krishna for his blessing before we begin to eat.**

(Hare Krishna trainee monk on a work visit to Glasgow with colleagues from the Krishna centre and eco farm in Lesmahagow)

******

Whatever its origin, Sabbatarianism once weighed heavily on human nature north of the Tweed. Not so many years ago, I have known of a Highland farmer refuse the loan of a girdle to bake scones for a breadless family, saying: "Not on the Sabbath."

(from the book "Bonny Scotland" by A.R. Hope Moncrieff, published in 1904)

"**E**lijah went into the wilderness where he lay down to rest under a furze bush. Then an angel touched him and said, *'Get up and eat.'* He looked around and there, at his head, was a scone baked on hot stones, and a jar of water."

(from the New Jerusalem Bible)

"The Scone also Rises"

I not only eat scones, I can make them because my wife taught me! I was brought up as a Christian in Pakistan and then became a Jehovah's Witness. My wife was Jewish, from Glasgow and we met in Pakistan after she became a Jehovah's Witness and was visiting Pakistan as a pioneer. We married and made our home in Glasgow and my wife's Jewish/Scottish heritage meant she was very good at baking. Our two sons and I learned how to make scones - plain, fruit and cherry - by watching her in the kitchen. My wife died while our boys were still at school but we've continued making scones - consulting her recipe books if necessary - and our 19-year-old has become particularly good at it. Everyone likes his scones!

(man giving out Jehovah's Witness literature, with a colleague, on Kelvin Way in Glasgow)

Fruit Scones: yea or nae?

Scones are probably our biggest seller
in the cafe, especially the fruit ones
which are always the first to go. You
can't go wrong with a scone. They're
popular with all ages. And we
sometimes have savoury scones in the
bar cafe upstairs, with olives and sun
dried tomatoes.

(Member of staff, Waterstones cafe)

******

*Four out of six people queueing at an
M&S cafe in Glasgow one afternoon
were treating themselves to a fruit scone
with butter and jam.*

(author observation)

I like scones. Cheese scones are good and easy to make. I like the smell when they've just come out of the oven. I used to meet up with a friend in Glasgow for a scone and a coffee. She preferred plain scones but if they only had fruit scones left, she'd get one and pick all the fruit out and then eat what was left of it - without butter.

(Karen)

******

I always have a pack of fruit scones in the freezer, just cheap ones from the supermarket, and when I fancy one, I heat it in the microwave for 30 seconds and have it with butter and lemon curd.

(Jim, retired bus driver)

I like a scone - a plain one with cream and strawberry jam and butter. I don't like the fruit ones. My auntie makes scones and she always has cream. Normally I'm a coffee drinker but with a scone, it has to be tea. Just talking about scones has put me in the mood for one! We had to make them at school but I've never made them since. But they're easy to make, aren't they?

(Stacey, cafe manager)

"Is it normal for a cat to like scones?"
(question on an internet forum)

We don't have treacle scones but we do have plain and fruit ones. Fruit scones are the most popular, although not with me - I don't like cooked dried fruit. I do make scones but I'm not a baker although I can cook. My mum's the baker in our family. I try to get my scones to rise as high as her's but they only get half way. My Fairy Cakes are pretty good now but they're easy to make.

(cheery waitress at a Foodfillas restaurant in Clydebank Shopping Centre where most of the tables were occupied by women eating fruit scones)

All Hail the Treacle Scone!
(the author's favourite)

I like a treacle scone, with lemon curd. But you need a good quality lemon curd, not a cheap brand. My son, who's 19, also likes treacle scones and is now a lemon curd convert.

(Male member of staff at Dobbies Garden Centre in Braehead who buys his scones from the food hall.)

My gran made delicious treacle scones. I make scones from time to time and the best thing about making your own is taking them out of the oven and eating them hot, spread with loads of Lurpak butter. Basically, it's butter with a scone.

(Phil, the good-looking florist)

******

My grandfather liked treacle scones which he pronounced *"trekle."* He was a miner, from High Blantyre (South Lanarkshire) which was pronounced, locally, *"Blantur"*.

(Alistair)

Oooh - I've not had a scone in a while; I haven't got the appetite for them now. But I used to love treacle scones. My grannie made delicious ones and, back in the day, cafes in Kilmarnock where I come from, always had a selection of scones on offer.

(Isobel, musician)

"Harry Potter and the Philosopher's Scone"

At Halloween, we'd go to my granny's and she had a pulley in the kitchen and they'd throw a long piece of string over the top of it and attach a scone and treacle to the end of the string and then all the kids would have a go at jumping up to try and get a bite of the scone - but you couldn't touch it with your hands - while somebody pulled the string up and away from you.

(Anne Marie)

We haven't had treacle scones in a long time. But we've started doing a nice treacle and fruit loaf which seems to be very popular. And cherry scones? We stopped doing those years ago. We've got plain, fruit and cheese.

(Staff member on the bakery counter at M&S in Glasgow)

"Cherry scones? I've never heard of those - they must be new."

"No - they're not. They've been around for years! You can get a very nice cherry scone in the M&S cafe."

(Two women friends, in their early 80s, sitting on a bench in Clydebank Shopping Centre, eating carry out chips from McDonald's)

The way to a man's heart is . . . scones?

"I have never made a scone in my life (save for one best-forgotten episode in domestic science) and have no intention of ever doing so. My husband, in the unlikely event that I ever find one, will have to go scone-less. Or get his scones elsewhere, ho ho."

(from the novel "Case Study" by Kilmarnock-born author, Graeme Macrae Burnet, 2021)

My mother, like many of her gender and generation, was an avid baker and made scones that, plastered with butter and smothered in jam, melted in the mouth. The humble scone, as everyone then knew, was why many men were drawn to a certain kind of woman. If a woman could bake the perfect scone, so received wisdom had it, then what couldn't she do?

(Scottish journalist, Alan Taylor, writing about his mother's scones)

******

I wish I'd done Domestic Science at school and learned how to make scones. But I had to do Latin instead.

(Anne Marie, retired teacher)

My first missus, she was good at making scones, I'll say that for her. When I was working in landscaping for the council, she'd make a batch of scones and put them in a poly bag for me to take to work. If I started eating one in the van, all the other boys would smell it and they'd want one, too.

(Tommy)

******

Men don't eat scones. It's ladies going shopping together who eat them.

(Colin, chess expert and scone refuser)

"Our baker is the best scone maker. You'd be hard pressed to find a better scone anywhere in Aberdeen. One customer said her husband was going to divorce her so he could marry the lady that made the scones!"

(Inverurie cafe owner, interviewed in the Aberdeen Press and Journal in 2022)

******

I've never met a man who would turn down a scone.

(Joyce, veteran scone maker)

I used to work with a guy who made very good scones that he'd bring in for us. Then he got a terminal illness and and when we went to visit him at home, he'd insist on getting out of his bed to make us scones, served hot from the oven with butter. That's the kind of man he was.

(Bill, retired engineer)

Scone Street near Possil in Glasgow

Scones at Scone (scoon)

Scone (scoon) Palace

Irn-Bru scone cooked in a frying pan

A scone at the Scottish Parliament

The Scone of Destiny with thanks to
Mischief La-Bas

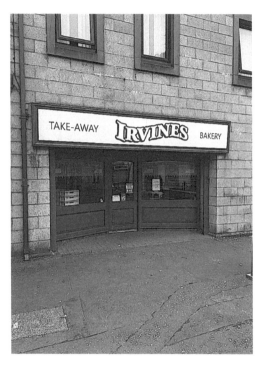

Irvines Bakery in Kilbirnie

A cheese scone at Fisher and Donaldson,
Dundee

A dainty scone baked by Christine of the
Sandyford Henderson Church, Glasgow

Charlie, the author's husband, living the
OAP dream at a cafe in Stirling, 2012

I like a scone and butter. My grannie made them - the ones with raisins. We had to make scones at school, in Milton, but they didn't come out the way I wanted. They were like rocks! You brought them home for your parents to try. Mine weren't impressed.

(Eddie, 60)

******

A properly made scone is a fine thing. Not that I can make them. I've tried in the past but they always ended up flat and hard - more like rock cakes.

(Madge)

I like a scone with jam and cream. I travel around the UK for business and that's what I usually have for breakfast at the hotels I stay in. I vaguely remember making scones in P7 at school in Govanhill, and bringing them home for my parents to try. I can't remember their reaction but they were from Pakistan and weren't familiar with scones.

(Mo, 50)

My granny made delicious scones: wheaten, plain and raisin but when she put a plate of mixed scones on the table, a wheaten one would be my first choice - with clotted cream but no jam. I've never liked jam. Of course you could get clotted cream in Scotland in those days! You could certainly get it in Giffnock where we lived.

(Winston)

I wouldn't go out and buy a scone
but if there's one on offer, I'll eat it
- as long as it's not a fruit one
because I don't like dried fruit. I'd
eat it with butter and jam. But
what's clotted cream?

(Andrew, 19)

******

*Isn't it just older people who
eat scones these days?*

(Ross, 37, charity worker)

I'm 20 and lots of people my age eat scones. It's true that many of our loyal, scone-loving customers are older women but we have one young guy who comes in regularly for a carry-out lunch and gets a sandwich plus a scone for dessert.

(cheery waitress working in Cranberry's Cafe in the Merchant City, Glasgow)

I eat scones regularly, for breakfast, or lunch . . . anytime. I think we made them in Home Economics but I use a recipe that I came across after I left school. I love baking and I make scones for the whole family; mostly plain - I have mine with butter and jam - but my mum also likes treacle scones.

(very nice teenage girl having a lunch break outside her mum's "Envy Hairdressing" salon in Beith, Ayrshire where she works)

I'm blessed where scones are concerned.

I make them myself; cheese are my favourite, eaten without butter; and I've made cheese and chive which are even nicer although I've yet to encounter them *"in the wild"* - in a shop. I live with my grandad because I moved up to Glasgow from down south to go to uni - I'm studying English Literature - and his neighbour has a catering business and makes scones which she gives me from time to time. She does blueberry and fizzy lemonade ones which are delicious! And I work part-time in a cafe where all the scones are made by the co-owner and if there are any left at the end of the day, I can take one home. I've had to start wearing a pedometer to counteract the scone effect!

(Jennifer)

******

My mum said she didn't feel entirely comfortable making scones until her mum - the supreme scone maker of the family - had died.

(Kirsty)

"We've always eaten scones in my family. My grandma makes scones but not my mum. She can't cook but she does buy scones, from a bakery, never a supermarket. I always eat a scone with cream and jam - the jam on first. How can you put the cream on first without it getting far too messy? And it has to be good jam and good cream."

(Katie, 23, Yorkshire-born, Glasgow-based artist and charity worker)

My mum wasn't at all the scone making kind of person - or any baking. I made scones when I was a teenager for my friends when they came over. They're dead easy. I just got the recipe from a book. But I didn't share them with my family. We all made our own food! I don't eat scones now. I gave up flour years ago - I'm gluten free.

(Lucy)

Not everybody eats scones
(shock horror!)

I'm not a big fan of scones. We learned how to make them at secondary school in Home Economics when we had to do a proper afternoon tea including setting the table with the cups and saucers, side plates and cutlery, making a pot of tea and baking the scones.

(Elaine, supermarket employee)

I'm not particularly keen on scones. Have I ever made them? No. I'd rather have "dough" in my purse than dough in the oven. I think I read that in the Beano or the Dandy.

(Anita, celebrity auctioneer)

******

Scones? I can take them or leave them. My auntie used to make fruit scones but I don't know if my mother ever made them because she died when I was six.

(man handing out Christianity leaflets in Buchanan Street, Glasgow)

I don't eat scones. We might have made them at school but that was a while ago. I'm at uni now, doing an English degree. My gran and my mum don't make scones because they're Polish and scones aren't part of Poland's food culture.

(Natalia, charity worker, Sauchiehall Street)

******

I was born in Scotland but my family background is Irish so my mum and my granny have never made ordinary scones - it's always been tattie scones.

(Michael, 22)

I'm Australian but I've got a Maltese/
Italian background and scones aren't
in our heritage but even though my
partner's parents are Scottish - they
emigrated to Australia when he was
four - neither of us had eaten scones
until we moved to Glasgow in 2019.
Now I'll have one occasionally but
Ciaran eats them all the time - for
breakfast, lunch . . . whenever. But
only with butter; he doesn't eat jam.

(Teri, artist)

I don't know anything about
scones. Nobody in our house
baked when I was growing up.

(Richard, 60)

A scone a day . . .

I'm not a scone eater. I did try making them during lockdown but I was so appalled at the amount of butter in them that I've never made them since - or eaten one.

(a Scottish cardiologist)

Note: *A basic scone recipe (according to the author's research) calls for as little as one to two ounces of butter or margarine (28 to 56 grams) per eight ounces (226 grams) of flour which doesn't seem an excessive amount of fat.*

"I know you can't stop people having coronaries and, as Ronnie said, she could have had it over a scone tea in Jenners' and everyone would have said, what a nice way to go."

(from "The Houseman's Trilogy" by Colin Douglas, 1985)

Jenners, a famous department store in Edinburgh, closed in 2020

******

You could choke and die eating a scone, they're so dry. In fact, I'd like to see the statistics for how many people choke on scones every year. No wonder they eat them with cream.

(Tom Brown, rickshaw driver and artist)

Conscious that a third of Europeans will be over 60 by 2030, Irish food scientists are developing novel, healthier formulations for scones. They believe these new scones can help address growing, global concerns about an overload of fat and sugar in the diets of elderly people who, the scientists point out, are regular consumers of scones.

(from a news report in the Irish Examiner, 2012)

I make scones, especially for my teenage grandsons who have huge appetites. I often make courgette scones, to get some veggies into them. I peel the skin off, so they don't notice, and then grate the courgette and use it like a liquid, along with less milk than you would normally add. And with butter and jam, they're fine!

(very obliging women in Beith, Ayrshire)

"A scone and yon"
(an Ayrshire expression?)

I met Jack and Margaret, a retired, married couple from Ayrshire, in the cafe at the Dick Institute in Kilmarnock. Jack said: *"Our daughter makes scones and she says they're dead easy and she's going to teach me."* Then Jack asked me: *"Have you heard the expression "a scone and yon"?"* At first I wondered if it was *"yawn"* - indicating that it might mean having a scone before you go to your bed at night - but eventually realise it's *"yon"* as in *"that - over there"*. We considered what it might mean but came to no conclusions.

I'm from Ayrshire but I've never heard the expression *"a scone and yon"*. But I've heard *"yer face looks like a right scone"* and *"what's up with yer scone?"* which mean roughly the same thing: *you don't look happy.*

(lovely woman working as a volunteer at the Heritage Centre in Beith, Ayrshire)

******

Jean and Hazel, both from Ayrshire, had heard the expression *"a scone and yon"* but weren't sure what it meant. Hazel recalled that her aunt used to say it in a way that implied it might be a euphemism for a snog, as in "having a scone - and a bit of a kiss and cuddle" (or just forget the scone element!).

Note: The author spoke to a number of people about the expression *"a scone and yon"* and we came to the conclusion that probably *"a scone and yon"* would be used when you were in a bakery or a cafe and were choosing what to have and you'd say *"I'll have a scone and . . . "* pointing to, for instance, a pancake or a doughnut *". . . and yon"* meaning "and one of those over there." An internet search came up with nothing, apart from a tea room in Inverurie, Aberdeenshire which was called *"The Scone and Yon"* but, sadly, has now closed down.

SCONE JOKE

A man goes into a branch of the City Bakeries and says, pointing to an item in the display case: *"Is that a scone or a meringue?"* And the shop assistant replies: *"No, you're no' wrang - that is a scone."*

(with thanks to Jane Barrie)

All these places, like garden centres, serve up what you might call "industrial" scones - they buy in a scone mix and add water. Supermarkets do it as well. It's just not the same as a scone made from scratch. Most of them don't even contain butter.

(Joyce)

******

The best scone I ever had was years ago at a cafe off Byres Road which I was in awe of until my friend Sally got a Saturday job there and revealed that they used a ready-made scone mix.

(Sarah)

I made the scones every morning at a cafe I worked in. We didn't use a mix - why would you when making scones from scratch is so easy? But we did grate the butter into the dry ingredients which saved time and energy.

(Martin)

If we're going on our own or with friends for a self-catering weekend away somewhere, I make up my own scone mix - rub butter into the flour etc., add some sultanas - stick it in a plastic bag and bring it with us so all I have to do when we come in from a walk is take the mix out of the fridge, add milk and maybe an egg to it and get some scones in the oven.

(Joyce)

I bake scones a couple of times a week, for my neighbours. One of them had 19 friends and family over recently and I made her a batch of almond and cherry scones. I can jot down the recipe for you if you want? I remember learning how to make scones at school in Airdrie and I've still got a Be-Ro flour booklet with a recipe for scones that I've had for decades.

(Wendy, retired school teacher, living in Pitlochry)

I'm from Newcastle and I do like scones, plain ones, with butter, jam - *Bonne Maman* for preference - and cream, in that order. I put the butter on the scone, then jam, then the clotted cream on top of that. You're saying clotted cream is like butter? That's controversial . . . ! If I make them myself, I use my mum's recipe. When she was a teacher, she'd bake scones on her birthday and bring them in for her colleagues.

(Claire)

Back in the late 1970s, I worked as a locum nurse/midwife in Shetland for a year - on Foula which is Britain's second most remote inhabited island - and the lovely woman I boarded with used to make scones when we'd run out of bread if the boat hadn't been able to get over to the mainland for supplies due to bad weather. She got really fed up with them but I didn't.

(Liz)

No offence to her but my mother's scones were really horrible. She'd produce them when we'd run out of bread. They weren't even like scones.

(Carla)

******

"**W**as going to make some scones yesterday because I'd run out of bread, and I was thinking: maybe cheese scones with a pinch of herbe de Provence? But then I couldn't be bothered."

(a text from Ann, trade union activist)

Domestic Goddess, Nigella Lawson says some of the best scones she's ever eaten had no sugar in them - useful if you suddenly find that you don't have enough bread in the house.

(from the internet)

******

If you can find me a scone without sugar, I'm sold! I think they're far too sweet.*

(Kiriyan)

*The author agrees with Kiriyan. Of the 25 scones she tried during her research - in 18 different cafes and bakeries in Scotland - many were too sweet. The recipe she has used (although not very often) for decades, from a Good Housekeeping book first published in 1969, contains no sugar.

******

Sticks and stones may break my bones but scones will never hurt me.

Email from Baroness Young of Old Scone (a Labour member of the House of Lords since 1997), kindly replying to one I had sent her, asking a variety of scone-related questions:

Deedee,

In fact, I love scones but mine tend to turn out flat and hard rather than deep and pillowy! My mother's were the same. I suffer from scone envy in respect of those who can make decent scones. The House of Lords serves ace scones and the baker down the road from where I live in England, called Bunty's Bakes, delivers sultana scones to die for.

The scone has of course been the bane of my life since I took the title Baroness Young of Old Scone. I had to get approval from my feudal overlord, the Earl of Mansfield, who owns the historic village of Old Scone from which my title derives (I was born there). He did warn me that people would call me an old scone and I didn't believe him but I now do! I have to explain that I am not an item of bakery goods. The coronation has helped as people learned about the Stone of Scone on which umpteen kings and queens have been crowned. They don't call that the Stone of Scon. Or the Stone of Scoan. It is the Stone of Scoon!

My sister and I did a sentimental journey to the town in Australia called Scone and were most upset that no-one knew the original Scone was in Scotland.

May not have answered all your questions but Old Scones forever.

Best wishes,

Barbara, Baroness Young of Old Scone

Asked what sort of business they'd consider setting up in a life after politics, Douglas Ross, leader of the Scottish Conservative Party, said he'd like to supply scones and other baked goods to the hospitality industry.

(from a news report in 2021)

******

SCOTS hunk Gerard Butler showed he enjoys a baked treat like the rest of us - after he ordered a massive batch of 60 scones to the set of his new film, *"Keepers"*, being shot in Stranraer and the Mull of Galloway.

(from a news report, 2017)

As an actor, you get some weird and wonderful jobs. One that springs to mind was playing the part of an egg in *"The Scone of Destiny"* for the outdoor theatre company, *Mischief La-Bas* where all the cast members dressed as scone ingredients and paraded a giant, fake scone through the streets of the towns we were performing in.

(Monica)

SO FAREWELL then, the *Great Tapestry of Scotland*, which for three weeks graced the entrance hall at the Scottish Parliament, pulling in an amazing 30,000-plus visitors. Presiding Officer Trisha Marwick revealed this week that there is a significant cross-over between a love of needlework and a taste for scones. Such was the demand for scones in the visitors' cafe, the parliamentary chef had to come in early in the morning and work a double shift to satisfy their craving.

(from "Unspun", the Herald's politics diary, 2013)

I'm working in the visitors' cafe while the Parliament is on holiday but I'm normally based in the MSPs restaurant and I can tell you, they love their scones! They're very popular with both men and women members.

(Kirsty, a member of the catering staff at the Scottish Parliament)

******

Scottish Government ministers spent more than £6,000 in two months on confectionery for guests and staff at its offices. The lowest spending offices were at the Marine Lab where the cost of 69 biscuits and seven home-baked scones was £46.99.

(from a news report, 2015)

"Mrs. Macnab was the wife of a farmer who lived near Ballater. Such was her reputation as a baker of scones that King Frederick of Prussia and other distinguished guests visiting Queen Victoria at nearby Balmoral, used frequently to go over and have tea with her."

(from "The Scots Kitchen", by F. Marian McNeill, published in 1929)

"This is pretty well a perfect scone; you'd pay a lot of money for that." Prue Leith praising Scottish actor, James McAvoy's cheese and chive scones on Celebrity Bake Off in 2021 (the episode where singer Anne-Marie revealed she'd never eaten a scone before.)

******

If Proust's aunt had eaten scones instead of madeleines for tea, *"A la Recherche du Temps Perdu"* would have been a very different book.

(from "A Caledonian Feast: Scottish Cuisine Through the Ages" by Annette Hope, first published in 1987)

Children and Scones

We all got a chance to make delicious, Scottish Irn Bru Scones! It's clear all the children are bakers in the making.

(news on the internet from Forth Primary School, South Lanarkshire)

******

My mother made scones and I can remember she used to recite a poem to me about scones - something about "butter running down poor Tom's face because he'd hidden a scone under his hat"!

(Joyce)

We do have baking sessions at Fair Isle Primary School which has a total of five pupils - two of them my own children who have learned to call me Mrs. Maxwell in the classroom and mum at home. Baking isn't my forte although I did make shortbread with the pupils. But we had a gran working at the school last year as a learning support assistant and she taught the children to make scones. Other grans and mums have come in for baking sessions and during one of these, the children made Halloween focaccia.

(Gillian Maxwell, head teacher at the UK's most geographically remote primary school, in Shetland)

When I was wee, before I was old enough to go to school, I spent a lot of time in the kitchen with my gran, helping her make scones which I think caused some concern for my father who was a traditional Highland man. My mum, on the other hand, was delighted with my baking!

(Angus, chef, who owns and runs Bodach's Kitchen in Glasgow with his wife, Janice)

******

My two sisters and I were encouraged to help my mum with the scone making from a very early age and on our tenth birthdays, we each received a Be-Ro recipe booklet from her so we could do our own baking.

(Robert)

SCONE FACTS

Scones are thought to have originated in Scotland in the early 1500s, with the first known print reference to scones made by Scottish poet - and bishop - Gavin Douglas in 1513.

(Two statues of Gavin Douglas can be seen in Edinburgh; one decorating the outside of the Scottish National Portrait Gallery and the other inside St. Giles Cathedral.)

******

Scone is a town in Perth and Kinross, Scotland with a population of 5,030 people, according to figures published in 2020.

(Wikipedia)

Scone is a town in New South Wales, Australia with a population of 5,624 people, according to the 2006 census.

(Wikipedia)

******

Scone is a locality in Ontario situated near the town of Chesley which was called Sconeville until a name change in 1868.

******

SCONE is the SCOttish Networking Event – an informal gathering of networking and systems researchers in and around Scotland, organised by the school of computer science at St. Andrews University.

(The author was unable to discover if scones are eaten at their meetings.)

SCONE is pronounced "skawn,"
as in gone.

******

Sconeisseur: an expert judge in
matters pertaining to scones.

(with thanks to V. O'Duffy)

******

*In the old days, when everyone
wore a hat, they'd call a man's flat
cap a **"scone"**.*

(with thanks to Brian)

Scone eating in Scotland
(according to the New York Times - in 1992)

"In Scotland, the scone isn't just a quick tea bread, it's a national institution. Although the English eat scones mainly at teatime, the Scots eat them at almost any time: with midmorning coffee, with soup and salad at lunch, at afternoon tea or high tea, *and even with a glass of wine at the cocktail hour.* Schoolchildren eat treacle scones as they swing along the street with their book bags, and commuters buy scones, the way New Yorkers might buy bagels, as they rush for their trains in Glasgow's Central Station."

Shakespearean Scones

"He is already named and gone to Scone." (Macbeth, Act 2, Scene 4)

******

"Ya wee scone!" - a supposed insult, hurled at police officers by a Scottish footballer during a late-night altercation outside a Glasgow pub. The 35-year-old later pled guilty at Glasgow Sheriff Court to behaving in an abusive and threatening manner and was fined £450.

(from a news report, 2016)

"Mad-Scone" was a New Word Suggestion submitted *(by someone based in Ireland)* to the Collins English Dictionary in 2012. It was described as: *"A term used to state that someone has acted in a manner which was not expected, such as when "someone has completed a relatively innocent simple act like standing up to their boss, or driving across a footpath."* A typical structure was stated as being: *"Ya mad scone!"* Approval Status for the word was listed as: *"Pending Investigation"*.

(from the internet)

A group of police officers on duty in Sauchiehall Street, Glasgow during the Cycling World Championships in August 2023 were asked whether you'd be more likely to find doughnuts or scones in a police station in Scotland these days. *"Definitely doughnuts"* they said. "If you went into a police station and saw scones, you'd wonder what was going on. It's all about a quick sugar fix; doughnuts are sweeter than scones and also a lot easier to eat."

Fun Fact: *In the official register of gifts donated to Police Scotland in 2019, items that were accepted included three packets of doughnuts and a selection of scones.*

The author decided to make some Irn-Bru scones, having come across a recipe for them on the website blog of the Robert Burns Birthplace Museum in Alloway (Ayrshire). In the post, from 2013, Museum staff attributed the recipe to Harry, a member of staff at the Ranald Hotel in Oban. I made my scones using a supermarket scone mix and an Irn-Bru "reduction" for the liquid. The result was okay but very sweet. I cooked one of the scones in a frying pan on the top of the cooker, in an attempt to produce a girdle scone. If I had used a heavier pan, on a lower heat, the result might have been better.

I remember scones being quite dainty things, when I was growing up. Now they're huge! I shared one the other day with a friend because it was too big for one person.

(Viv)

******

You get giant scones at the garden centre in Angus where I come from. They're as big as cow pats.

(Neil, 36, photographer)

******

I am a great fan of scones and give marks out of ten for each one devoured.

(Anne, East Kilbride, from an email)

"**My** daughter says you can interview her in-laws who are huge scone fans. They travel for scones. Audrey likes a cheese scone with jam and Doug is a fruit scone. They were so bereft during lockdown they made their own but have now resumed travel and eating scones. They discuss flavour and price."

(Iain, from a text)

******

My sister is quite serious about her scone eating and gives cafes marks out of ten depending on the quality of their scones.

(from a text)

One of the best scones I've ever eaten was at the Calanais Standing Stones cafe when I was visiting Harris in the Outer Hebrides. I told the staff how impressed I was and they called through to the kitchen for the baker who turned out to be a boy of about 16! He very kindly gave me the recipe and I've used it ever since.

(Patricia)

******

I've eaten scones in some far-flung places including one in Oaxaca, in Mexico. It was very good!

(Paul, manager of AllSaints in Glasgow. His colleague, Faisal, also likes scones.)

Do they make scones in England? Or is it just in Scotland?

(Charlie, the author's husband who turned out to know less about scones than she realised)

About Deedee Cuddihy

Deedee Cuddihy is a journalist who was born and brought up in New York but has lived in Glasgow since the "Big Storm" of 1967 (which she slept through). Or was it 1968? After finishing art school in Glasgow, she realised being an artist would be too difficult - and being an art teacher would be even more difficult. So she became a journalist and has been one ever since. She is married to a Scotsman and has two grown up children - plus four granddaughters. "I Love Scones" is the 18th in her Funny Scottish Books series, the other titles including the best-selling "I Love Irn-Bru", "The Wee Guide to Scottish Women" and "Only in Dundee". She thinks all scones produced by Irvines Bakery are delicious - especially the treacle ones.

**Other books by Deedee Cuddihy in
the Funny Scottish Books series:**

How to Murder a Haggis
I Love Irn-Bru
Only in Dundee
The Wee Guide to Scottish Swearing
I Love Tunnock's Tea Cakes
The Wee Guide to Scottish Women
The Wee Guide to Porridge
Scottish Sweetie Addicts
Under the Skin of the Scottish Tattoo
Scottish Wedding Disasters
I Love the West End (of Glasgow)

Further information about the series
and to order copies:
www.funnyscottishbooks.co.uk